THE EXTRAORDINARY LIFE
OF AN ORDINARY MAN

THE EXTRAORDINARY LIFE
OF AN ORDINARY MAN

Paul Ramsden

Trafford rev. 01/06/2011

 www.trafford.com

North America & international
toll-free: 1 888 232 4444 (USA & Canada)
phone: 250 383 6864 ♦ fax: 812 355 4082

I WAS INTO citizens band radio communications all my life. My sister in law had the perfect base station location. However, I was not happy with the antenna location and decided it was time to relocate it. I was drinking beer there were many high voltage lines in that area, I told the people that were with me that we did not need to drop the antenna onto those lines. We dropped the antenna, no one was shocked so we went back and up onto third floor roof. We then began putting ant into its new location. We got base plate in place and put tower mast and ant in place, had two guidelines in place, and told Ed to go down hook put cable to base station antenna. Ed called back on a walkie-talkie and said reception was 100percent and told him to come back to hook last support wire and that the wind had really picked up. I bean walking to where we were to hook up last tie down cable. The ant fell over onto the high voltage transmission line, which carries 14,000 volts of a c current. Since I was drunk did not worry about my safety and pulled ant off wire. I was walking down to attach guide wire when wind took the ant over that dam high voltage line again. I tried in vain but the antenna felt glued to the line, and would not budge. My body was shaking while all this was going on but with all the booze, I was not worried about myself, but I was worried about what happened to my sister in laws house. Than ant on wire sounded like swarm of bees around their hive. I do not remember how I got off the roof. I ate some pizza while waiting to for the ambulance to arrive. I went to the Lewistown hospital and spent one week there. I was told by Doctor Brown that I Would have died if I had not been drinking beer because my body was related with the booze's had knocked all electric in beaver springs area. The surge blew all the glass out of all the fuses in meter box. It blew all wall sockets out burnt the citizens band and power supply to a crisp. There was also smoke coming out of the wall sockets. Now here is what my life was like. I was born into an average family. However, my life was not that stile of life. I would skip school when I had chance. Was always in fists fights some won some lost a lot was broken up. Had many girl friends some of which were great some not. Had first sex with a girl at ripe old age of twelve and it was very good? I began drinking beer at that age also. When I reached my eleventh year at high school dropped out and joined the U. S. Army. I took up field wiremen course. It was very interesting and I learned a great deal. as a advanced in the army and went from post to post began fixing radios that were not transmitting or receiving and made them right. I went to Germany, had lots of fun, and met many interesting people. I began drinking beer and whiskey while there. I had reenlisted four yrs, prior to this and I was in until the war in Viet Nam ended. I found that I did not like outfit I was with and put in transfer to Viet Nam. I was giving green light and went to Cam Rahn Bay Viet Nam. I went to a military police outfit and later went to Nha Trang where I stayed for reminder of time there. I had exposure to the chemical Agent Orange while I was over there. I had had rocket and mortar attacks and small arms fire very often. I did a lot of traveling throughout South Vietnam. I saw many bridges and stuff that the Viet Cong or the nva Soldier's munitions blew apart. All the time there worked on radios and telephones.

Well I am back; again, I had to take a day off to do some relocating information. I am going to go back some years. I had many friends when I was growing up and would like to share some of those. My very best friend his name was Silvio he was more like me. We went for long walks exploring old coalmines; some closed off due to the deep water and darkness. We went into many caves in our travels. We played many tricks on each other while in there. We would find dumps and go through all the junk looking for treasures, one time we found a can; it had some unknown stuff in it. We took that can to Silvios home and went into his basement. Silvio put the can on the stove and turned on gas after about five minutes this black thick smoke began rolling out and filled the cellar with smoke. It was not long before the smoke to go up stairs and for his parents started raising hell. That was the last can we ever put on that stove. One time we found an old motor home in woods and there were signs that owners were away a long time. The door was unlocked so we went in and found many treasures Silvio used to build shacks in woods and kept comic books and many other things hid in there. We spent many hours in there telling stories and having parties. In the winter, we would sled ride and make trains. I was always going home with cuts and scratches. In those days, cars were scars and could go on many roads we no fear of being run over. The older teens would build long bobsleds with steering wheels on, us longer kids never go to ride with them. They would go to top of hills and roads and would holler look out below, and down they would coming roaring past us. Most of the time the older kids smashed up before that got to us. Most of the time we had a big roaring fire going to get warm and dried up, it was such fun.

One on the many things we would do would be to divide a bunch of kids into two equal groups. One group would fill their pockets with crab apples, get a switch from a tree, and put a point on the stick. The group in the woods would hide behind whatever they found. After a short while, the other group came into the woods looking for us. It then was all out war trying to hit others with the apples, after that we would change and we would get to find the others that were hiding. It ended with many black eyes etc. We also had snowball battles, mud ball battles and rock battles. I really liked when the girls fought. They kicked; bit pulled each other's hair and name calling such fun. The fights I was in were fiercer than the girls were. My parents taught me to respect girls. No matter what the girls was always right big deal? In junior high school, I took up wood shop. I have to use power machines and made lamps and things. When I was in high school took up machine shop. Made many things some of which I was not to do put you know boys. Made a set of dies out of stainless steel was a real challenge trying to roll those babies. Took a starter gun into shop took it apart and bored out barrel and cylinder and could shoot 22 caliber shorts. Was all right until my grandfather got wind of what I had done. That was the end of the gun gramps took the gun away and that was the end of that. Another time Silvio and I were damming up a creek and I found an old roust 45 caliber had gun in the creek bed. I tried to get the damn thing to fire but there was just too much rust. We would play cops and robbers until gramps again heard of my find. Gramps took the handgun to his work, cleaned, and took it apart. One bullet was in position ready for firing and four bullets had already shot. Gramps told me the gangsters in New Kensington most likely used gun in a murder. That was the end of the handgun, and I never asked another question about it. Not long after that, we found a one o five howitzer shell casing with no persisted in it just the cap and a long tube with a screw in the end with powder in it. We turned that shell upside down and beat on it with rocks but could not get it to go off. Yes, you guessed it, gramps found out about it and again took it to work, and he gave it back to me minibus the cap. He had cut a two or three inhale around cap and removed it. After that the fun and excitement was over. My mother's parents were very close to me. I went fishing and hunting with my grandfather. I was the son they did not have. My grandparents bought a piece of ground near Tionesta in northern Pennsylvania. We all pitched in a built a cabin there. The hunting and fishing were unbelievable. I went on long walks in woods with Elmer my grandfather. In addition, he taught, me many interesting things about nature and all its beauty. We would find many types of mushrooms, which we would clean, and my grandmother Rose would prepare for us to eat. We also went fishing at many of his choosing areas and again my grandmother Rose would fry them for all to eat. We would cutout-unwanted trees, build a fire, and sit around talking about just about anything that came to mind. Sometimes we roasted hot dogs sometimes it was marshmallows. If we could not dig out stumps, grandpa would buy dynamite and we would blow them out, what fun that was. We would go to the cabin and stop at a hardware store on the way and gramps had to tell Rose his wife that he was buying a hammer so she would not know that there was ten pounds of dynamite in the trunk. Am going to stop now and see what is on the boob tube.

Well here it's Monday January 12, 2004. What am I going to tell you all today. Have many health problems, and hope I am able to finish my book. Am going to tell about my trip to Korea 1965. Went to South Korea by ship and took about twenty-five days. We had about the best chow that a person could eat. Watched movies when weather aloud. Played cards told stories or just sat there daydreaming. We had a two submarine escort the whole way across Pacific Ocean. One day I was sitting on deck and heard this loud thump and felt the vibrations through the deck someone hollered look over the side we hit a submarine. Found out later submarine was coming to surface and sort of bumped our ship. Neither ship nor submarine reported any damage. We were very close to where food was stored and had many days of free fruits. We made a drink from pineapples, had the shits for two days, and were end of that idea. The telephone is ringing again but is not going to answer it because I know it is my daughter's husband at work. I met many people on the ship. There were three thousand soldiers on the ship not counting navy crew, officers and Wacs Army women or personnel. We had a dead admiral that was in the safe. He requested his burial to be at sea between Guam and Hawaii the captain had to change plans because the body started to smell. They slowed ship to a halt almost stop and had a big deal about it because that is what death is all about. After funeral was over, the captain got the ship going again. We made stop in Guam for fresh fruits and supplies and off we went again. When our ship left harbor we pasted under the famous Golden Gate Bridge that was a great day in my history. I am going to stop for a while to think about what to talk about.

Was out working on my son in laws car and had many things to repair. There is something wrong because the damned thing just will not start. My son in law Raymond is waiting for parts to get here tomorrow. It is going to snow tomorrow into the next day and hope we get them into car before the snow starts, ha ha.

My wife has to work today and tomorrow so my daughter Jean is driving mother's car taking mother back and forth to work. I am disabled and nobody but nobody is going to drive my truck. Am going to have birthday next month and I will be fifty-eight years old. Moreover, I will be fifty-eight years old, an old F—k ha ha. I Have to be careful of what I eat haha. Its hell getting old I am so used to fishing, hunting, and chasing wild women haha. I never wrote a book before but if this one sells, may write another only time will tell. There was a time when my friend Silvio and I bought about fifteen pounds of carbide. Many people do not know what carbide is. Coalminers used it on their headlamps. The way they did that carbide went in one place, water went into next compartment, they inter mixed with other and left off a gas, you would light this with a tool, and a bright light would shine. My friend Silvio and I decided to make some noise by making a bomb. We found an old five-gallon can with lid and put a hole in bottom. Then added about three handfuls of carbide and poured water onto the carbide, gas fumes began coming out and we placed lid onto can. The gas fumes began coming from hole and told my friend Silvio to find piece of paper, light it and put lighted paper under hole as you might expect I had can between my legs to balance it. There was a very large bang, lots of smoke. I rolled over top of Silvio, and we lay very still for very long time.

After what seemed an eternity, we began moving and everything was out of focus for a very long time. Could not hear or see for long period. When we gained our composer back began laughing aloud and said we would not do something as stupid as this ever again. Without my friend, Silvio my life would have been less exciting. One time Silvio was working on a car, changing motors around souping it up. I walked over to see what he was doing and asked him if he had hooked up motor mounts and he said for me to mind my on business. He hooked up battery cables, climbed in car, and fired it up. Guess what Silvio forgot to hook up hold down supports and engine jumped forward right through radiator, I never said a word just turned and went home thinking boy what a dumb ass Silvio is. He and I were into everything, never worrying about things that could happen to us, until it was too late. I lost my best friend Silvio at a very young age of nineteen. He was in basic training and heard many stories that he was eating chicken and chocked to death over a bone in his throat. I have the idea that he had a seizure and that was cause of death. I went home for his funeral. Wouldn't you know they buried Silvio a week before. His parents took their hurt out on me, since I was also in the army. One time Silvio built this huge wagon, had a steering wheel inside, and always needed someone to push the damned thing. I asked Silvio if I could get inside and was told later. Later turned into never and I put and end to that real fast. I said I am sorry I feel sick and went home and that cured Silvio very fast. There was this time he bought this Whizzered bike and could not get the engine to fire. I again had to push this thing and still it would not start. I asked if I could try it and was refused. There was a real long hill and told Silvio to head down hill, which Silvio did, again

I went home and that was end of that and not a word was said. Silvios dad made sand and cinder blocks and we would play for hours in the sand pile. Would dig tunnels and use Popsicle sticks to hold them up. Silvios dad would go to make blocks and find those sticks in the sand and forbid us from playing in sand but would do it just to piss off his old man.

Here is another thing that Silvio and I did in our travels. We were on a long walk out in the deep woods and came upon this old school bus and no body was around it. We had a hard time prying open the rusty door but soon were inside. Found old newspapers, old broken objects and near the back under a bunch of junk found three boxes of shotgun shells, which I put inside my pants pockets. Yes as you might already guess went to Silvio's home and into the basement we went. I told Silvio we were going to make cannon. We located a pipe three quarters by about sixteen inches in length. I drilled a hole near the metal cap that was on one end. Next I poured the powder into pipe and then added wading then the bb's then more wading and then drove a piece of wood in end and now were ready to try out our cannon. Had no fuse so we used a match with the sulfur end in pipe, put cannon on a cement post, and lighted the match but it kept going out and so I turned the pipe over with the match pointing down and lit the match. On about the fifth attempt success, that was one hell of a flash and bang. We found our cannon but the end where that wooden plug was, the pipe looked like an open flower. That was the last time we foiled around with cannons.

There was this time when some of my other friends and I had a very interesting time. In those days there was not many cars on the roads and gathered up all kinds of shit trees, logs and cans and closed off the road. After awhile heard, this car coming down and we all hid in different places. The driver stopped his car, got out, used some very choice words, threw things everywhere got back in car, and took off down the hill. After some time we all met back on road and one person was missing. I called out his name and way off heard him respond. Here he was inside this drainage pipe covered with most of our barricade and had to dig Chuck out. Where I grew up there was three roads that came up to where we lived and only two roads would the city maintain . . . We had a large area we play sports on. We would make fires and sit around telling ghost stories and other tells.

When I was growing up there, were no blacks around they all had their own schools, churchs, and place to live. I went to eight grades and that is when the blacks began to show up. I played football and basketball with them, had many black friends, and could never figure why they were treated cruelly harshly. When I was on a plane going to Viet Nam a black soldier said to me hang out with the brothers and you will come home in one peace and damned if he wasn't right, thanks to all the blacks in my outfit.

You are probably asking whys this clown writing this story and it has to let other people know what took place in my life. I thought about all this and thought hell this is history this is my life. It is some of the many interesting things that made up my life and want to share them with my readers. Right now its eleven o'clock pm and it's snowing outside. My daughter Jean went to my wife Jane's' work to pick here up and thought lets get back to my story. Never wrote a book before and there is many UN answered questions that need answered. Am going to public library tomorrow to get some literature about writing a book, which I am going to use.

When I was in the United States Army I took basic training at Fort Jackson South Carolina I met a lot of fellows from all parts of America. The training they put a fellow really helps make a man out a boy. We had to leave Pittsburgh, Pennsylvania by train to get to training center at Jackson. There was a fellow by the name of Tom Risbon that was in my car. Tom said he wanted to shave before train began to move but that did not happen. Tom filled washbasin with water put shaving cream and thought he was all set. Just about, the time Tom put razor to his face the train began moving. Tom washed the soap from his face, left water out of sink, three times this happened to poor Tom, and he decided that he wasn't meant to shave and give up that idea. There was another fellow by the name of Albert Juke's that was with us. We were always called the big three, we were inseperatiable, where one was the other two were always near. We had many train stops along our trip and once the train was on one set of tracks, out in the middle of nowhere' and the train stops and stayed there for what seemed hours. After we got to Columbia, South Carolina, we were loaded into buses and taking to the fort. Had tons of papers that needed filled out and then our bedding was handed out to our entire group. I told Tom and Al that after to they showed us how to make our beds we were going to go to bed, that was a joke. We were sent out in formation, said they had a job for us, and asked for volunteers and I raised my hand as well as Tom and Al. We were on our way to the mess hall for kitchen police big damned; deal. That was the last time I ever volunteered for anything. When at Fort Jackson we were up near tank hill and could see most of the fort but that was short lived. I was at the fort for nine weeks and there were parts of the fort we never have to see. One day I was out walking, caught a field mouse, took it back to the barracks, and told some people in there what I was going to do. I pulled back blanket on Toms' bunk and placed the mouse under his sheet. I then took light bulbs that were over his bunk out. After some time in walks Tom and wants to write, a letter and I told him to get undressed, go to bed, and write his letter the next day. After some doing, he did what I suggested. Tom slid under covers and all of a sudden he turns all different colors and I ask him what's' wrong. Tom says something is in his bed, its; moving and its furry and he's' not sleeping in that bed. I then caught the poor mouse and put it outdoors, I told Tom okay go to bed and he refused to sleep in that bed so I had to give Tom all my bedding and take his and then we all went to bed. We did all kinds of things to Tom and many others of our friends. Hell if you would ever do that to someone these days they would pull out a handgun and shoot somebody. One time we went into this building to clean it and were told not to let anyone in. All was okay until we went into another room. Tom said how are we to clean these back rooms with doors unlocked and I said hell that is easy. We pushed this great big table against the doors and that solved our problems boy was I wrong. That just started bigger problems because someone that worked there had night business that had to be taking care of and I refused to move the desk. I really thought world war three was going to start but after sometime got everything taking care of.

Today were going back to Germany to learn some more facts about my life. I was in Germany the year of 1966 but was satisfied with the unit I was with but will talk about that later. Was on guard duty with another fellow soldier and it was an ammo dump we were watching. There was this very large tent with all kinds of things inside. Yes. As you can already figure out things were about to get very interesting but could have been very deadly for both of us. I found a device that is used to set off land mines. I told this fellow soldier lets take one of these devices, walk down road a small ways, and rig the device across this road, which we did. About this time, we hear this vehicle coming up the road towards us and we jumped over wire that closed off the road into ammo dump. I told this person we would go hid inside the tent and no matter what happens we are not going to come out of that tent. All the German trucks have automatic transmissions and when the truck ran over trip wire a loud bang rang out and this German soldier locked up all the wheels. Such a racket, the truck stopped and out jumps this German soldier with his pistol in hand. I said to the guy with me go out and ask the German soldier if he needed any help and the guy with me told me to go f—k myself.

There was this time we were guarding the natal site and all hell broke loose. This American soldier on the very last guard post starts shooting at the finch near him and now we are put on a red alert, and after the higher ups find out whets going on all clear is giving. What started all this was a wild boar was digging a hole under the finch and this guard shot to scare the boar away. One time I was chosen to go along with a radio and my forty-five pistol. We were told what were to do under different circumcises, here we are in these trucks out on this supper high way going as fast as this truck could go. All of a sudden, we stop and they yell fire and that means clean everyone out of the area, which

I tried in vain there, was the language barrier and people just kept doing what they wanted to do. Then all clear was giving and into the truck, we go. We were told we had nukes in drums and were taking them to another location. After a great while people around me asked when are we going to make a piss stop and I told them hell just piss out back of truck. It can be done but you will stand there looking stupid for a very long time until you poss. should know it happened to me many times.

The NATO sight was the only place we had to pull guard duty for weeks at a time. I liked guarding the ammo dump because I got to pet some of the guard dogs. There were two dogs that were to mean to touch so I just talked to them. When the dog owners were around there was no way even getting close to the dogs. I spent much time watching the handlers training their dogs. The guards had dogs that would patrol the wire perimeter by them selves. The dogs would keep changing directions while they were making there rounds. When we were not guarding different locations, we would be doing other things, like playing war games. The sirens would sound and away we would go. One night a bunch of us was in the village drinking booze and this truck came through blowing his horn. We ran out of this place and driver said we were on a red alert and into the truck, we pilled. Were back to company area got all our gear and put in truck, and I went to communication room and got my radio and handset. After we were to our destination had to get book, go on air, and get radio comm . . . set up. The radios where a real pain in the ass getting radio set on frequency before able to transmit. I found this bunker and slid down inside and got set up and after a few minutes was told come on the alert has been cancelled. I later found out that the battalion commander got drunk and pushed alert button by mastake. There was another time I was drunk and went out on this alert, which became very interesting. My friend Dave carried what we called a stovepipe (rocket launcher) and I helped to carry some of his equipment. We were loaded inside this banana shaped chopper, were flying over this rice paddle, and were told to jump out. Was about two feet above this rice paddy and when I jumped, missed the path, landed down in the rice paddy itself, and needed help being pulled out?

At night, the North Koreans would play propaganda music and such to us. They told us what a great place it is to live in North Korea. Every so often would go guard this bridge, which were we on one side and the North Koreans on the other side. At night while on duty anything that was half ways across the river was free game, you just shot and did not worry. Every night this tank would come out after dark and set up a position near the water not far from bridge. They had a large spotlight mounted right under the big gun and would shine the light out across the river every so often.

When I was younger, mom and Tom would take me to an amusement park called Kenny wood and we would be there all day long. They had four roller coasters that we would ride all day long. They also had this ship called Noeas' Ark and I spent most of my time here. There was all kinds of rides and games to play and would spend many hours at each one of them. All the roller coasters were on wooden frames and would go about ninety miles an hour in the evenings. Many years later when I was in the army there was a big fire and do not know if the park is still open now.

When I was growing up my cousin Danny worked at a carnival and I have to ride all rides free, it was much fun. I always felt sorry for Danny because he had polio when he was younger and was always in such pain but eventually he grew up and the pain is gone but he has a brace on his foot.

When I was younger was in the boy scouts, went to many camps, and had much fun. One time we went to this camp and my friend and I have to carry all the food and keep it near our tent. It rained all day and part of the following day and we built a fire to make breakfast. We had a big pot and mixed everything we could find together. The so-called top scouts could not get their fire started and asked me if they could use the fire I had going and I told them no. I said to them they would not let me use their fire so they had to make their own but after awhile I told they go ahead and use the fire.

There was another camp we was at called Tionesta Boy scout Camp and had interesting things that took place. The first day we were there, I went to the camp store, bought a candy bar, and threw the wrapper on the ground. I was caught and this fellow said come here and got my name and unit I was with. This person gave me this five gallon can and told me to fill it with trash I found around camp. When I got the can filled and went back to camp store this fellow checked to see if the can was full. I went back to my campsite, the instructor there gave me all kinds of hell, and that was last time I threw anything on the ground.

I wanted to take a canoe out on Tionesta creek but since I could not swim, was not aloud use of the canoes, what a bummer that was. A lot of the training I learned in scouts helped me later in life. There were many things the scouts did that I wanted no part of so I was not with them very long. They said one thing, turned around, and did the things anyways.

Before I got out of the army, I bought this Honda motorcycle and had much fun. I used to go to this cycle shop and Marty the owner told me I could trade my cycle for this Harley sprint, which I did. One time me and this other fellow went to the fire hall which he was a member. I told this fellow the road this way was shorter than this other road and started out to prove I was right but something was about to happen. It had been raining and road was slippery and when I went around this bend lost it. After some time lying on road got up and restarted motor. As I was going down the road, my headlight was facing up into the trees on the right side of the road. I also was proving wrong that my way was shorter.

My grandparents had this cabin up near Tionesta and told Elmer that I was going to cabin Friday so I would have it nice and warm when they got there. It was very cold riding up to the cabin and after going about thirty miles turned around and back home, I went. When I got home Tom, my stepfather told me that my grandparents had gone to the mountains. The next morning left for the cabin but had to stop many times to be warmed up. When I finally have to cabin got warm, went hunting with my grandfather Elmer, and made out very good so it was not wasted time after all.

I spent many wonderful times with my grandparents and traveled to many places with them. I went with them to California and many other states and had such fun with them. Hope when I die that I get to be with them again. I spent more time with my grandparents than I spent with my parents.

I had another friend by the name of Fred and I went down to his home and he said lets go into the basement. Fred had this old double-barreled shotgun and wanted to make it into a sawed off shotgun. We found a hacksaw, cut off the stock and barrels, and wanted to shoot the thing to see what would happen. We got some shells, went down behind his home, and loaded up the gun. Fred asked me to shoot and I gave the honors to Fred. He pulled back the hammers and pulled one trigger and that was the end of that, the gun flee out of his fist and Fred thought his wrist was broken. After that, Fred never played with any firearms.

This one Christmas Fred got a short wave radio that had to solder together which I helped from time to time to put it together. Fred knew this ham radio operator by the name of Robert and had him check for mistakes, which he found many and corrected them. After some time Robert plug the radio in and fired it up, it worked very well.

There were many times we would go to see Robert and he left us talk to other ham radio operators around the world. There was this time Fred said he knew where we could buy two radios and set up two base station antennas. They only had one channel but had hours of fun with them.

My grandparents had this home in the country, I went over to see the neighbors, and he had some citizen band radios for sell and bought one. The radio had three channels 5, 7, 9 and came with rabbit ear antenna. I would talk to another friend of mine by name of Mike Gross who lived about eight miles away. Mike had a base station radio that had twelve channels which he put this gismo onto the radio and could add whatever channels he desired. The antenna he had been a ground plane antenna up on the chimney. One time Mike and I went to bear electric and we bought the walkie-talkies that had to be put together. This one night Mike said go walking around with walkie-talkie and he would use the base station radio to keep in touch. After some time I decide to go to this restaurant to get a coke and keep in touch with Mike. Was sitting at this booth when all of a sudden three black limousines pulled up out back and stopped and out got two men. After sometime, this person comes in and comes over where I was sitting, looked around, and found a place to stand. About that time, this other person comes in and stands over next to back door. Then two more people all in black suits comes in and sits at counter and ordered coffee. As I sat there wondering what the hell this was all about heard the one guy say how do you like my new ring and the other guy said yea it's very nice. The first person said he bought it for ten thousand dollars cash. I told Mike about this and he came down we also found out that these people were part of the Sam Manarino gangsters.

One time I was in the basement talking to Mike on radio and came up with a brainstorm. I got these two backpacks put car battery in one and the transceiver radio in the other pack and then hooked steel whip ant 108 inches to one of the packs. I then called Mike by phone and advised him I was all set. Went back down stairs, put everything on, and out the garage door I went and called Mike by radio it was doing a great job. I guess everyone that say me probably thought I had flipped, but I was having such fun.

There was another time we took our walkie-talkie radios and heading for boa k mts., which we walked to. We climbed the mountain and went through narrow passageways to reach our destannation. Once we got to where we wanted to be in side a cave I crawled through this upper crevice and hooked the radio cable in a large tree and ran the wire back into the cavern and hooked wire to radio. We had very good reception, talked into many states, and really had much fun.

I was on top of boe k hill one time with Fred and we went over and talked to the people that operated the KDKA radio antennas and equipment. The one person told me they would pay us five hundred dollars if we would climb the towers and paint them. I said we would but this other fellow said no so that was the end of that deal.

When I got the transceiver, radio there was no outside antenna so I was using rabbit ear antenna. I had many old radios, took the transformers out, and took them apart. I had a big roll of wire, was trying different things for antennas, and hooked up this ball of wire and wouldn't you know it worked very well. The next antenna I got was a ground plane antenna, which was hooked to the chimney on the roof.

When we went to visit family members in Scottdale, Pennsylvania would put radio in Tom's car and always had many wires lying all around. I talked to many others and got many radio cards from people I talked to from other parts of the country. I collected cards from just about every state in the US and also some other country also listened to short wave radio, was member with call sign WPE 3 FCN, and received call cards from around the world.

My wife's parents live in Snyder County and that is where I did all my hunting. When I was working would leave home so that I could go either deer hunting or small game hunting. When

I first started hunting everyone was still alive and would hunt until around twelve noons, go back to the house and eat either chili or homemade soup. After hunting was over, we would clean and wash the game and put in freezer. We would rest up abet then change clothes and go to the VFW club, this went on many years until John my brother in law called everyone in Columbia and said no one could afford going out any more and that was the end of that. My sister in law Joy was really pissed at John for a very long time.

My father in law had this truck and said to convert it over into a deer-hunting vehicle. My brother in-law John and I took measurements of inside of vehicle and went to lumber company a bought all the materials we need to put bunk beds in the back. After we were done, we loaded all our bedding and hunting gear and food into truck. We then drove the up on mountain behind the house and got everything set up. That night my brother in law Smitty brought this heater up but had to put it out because, it was giving off dangerous fumes which we thought would kill us. The next morning when we woke, it was so damned cold in there that nobody felt like hunting. Smitty went and bought this other heater and the same thing happened. John said lets get a kerosene heater and try that, it is worked just right, and we all were very happy. I shot many deer at this location but this was short lived.

One year we decided to go bear hunting and borrowed a camper but had to fix the flat tires first. I pulled the camper with my nieces pick up truck to her house. We loaded all our gear in and away we went to a private hunting area on the side of the mountain. We sat up most of the night drinking beer and telling stories. In the morning out we went and picked are own areas to hunt. After it got day light Randy hollered for me to go over where he was hunting and under these logs was a head of cow that a bear had dragged up there to eat, Randy said lets walk through the woods looking for the deer which we did. Some time later Freedom comes along and said, let us go eat lunch. When we reached, the camper Freedom set up this target and everyone fired his or her rifles twice. I decided to shoot my rifle and guess what I had forgotten to put a bullet into the chamber.

The first day of bear hunting, we decided going on top of Jacks' mountain and began driving up a mountain road that was end of rough trip. The snows on the roads keep getting deeper and we kept going. The last road we had to go up was very rocky and steep and got to a place where the truck just could not go so I asked Freedom to take over the driving and he said okay. He would go forward then go into reverse and kept sliding closer to his edge of road. He was at the point of rolling truck over mountain when he decided to hook winch from this little Toyota to his big truck after some fancy maneuvers they got the truck back on road. I climbed back into truck and we backed down the road and soon found a place where we could get both trucks off road. We decided to hunt where we were and away we went. After walking a great distance, I told Freedom I was going to sit and let the nuts run the mountain and I sit and wait for their return, which I did. The snow was up over my knees and made it very difficult walking. After awhile I went back to truck, saw a log, and thought I would sit there but when I sat down my ass slid off and there I was lying on my back. I had one hell of time getting off that log, had to roll over on my side . . .

The last day we decided going on top of Shade Mountain to hunt bear. This road is about thirteen miles from one end to the other and during winter months, it is not plowed. there was deep grooves from other four wheeled drive vehicles going through and Freedom we would have no trouble and on I drove. We were about eight miles out and got between two hills where the truck just would not go. Freedom said he would walk out for help and it was about four in the afternoon. I would sit till I got cold and then fire the engine to warm truck but had to watch because there was only a quarter of a tank of fuel. At about ten, that night saw headlights coming towards me and it was Freedom with two four-wheel drive vehicles. After what seemed forever, we got the truck back on the main road. My niece had to pay eighty dollars and was she ever pissed at us. That was the end of our bear hunting and no bear.

Yesterday my stepdaughter gave me hell and her and Ray stayed in their room all night. Today Ray told my wife he would stay in his room as long as the old man (Paul) was at home. My wife Jane started on me and I started getting chest pains, went in, and lay on our bed. Jane told Ray she was not going to work because of my pains. Therefore, Ray and Jean took off. After they left, I came out and got into a real mouth battle with Jane and she went into bedroom. Afterawhile I finally talked her into going to work which she did but did not talk to me at all in my truck. There is bad weather moving into our area tonight and hope I can get Jane home before the snow gets here. We live about ten miles from York and there are many hills to go up. I am a nervous wreck when there is snow on our roads.

I have had many narrow escapes in snow and it worries me driving in snowy weather. Since I am disabled, I do not go out driving when the roads are bad but will have to tonight. Today is Sunday and it is going to snow all the way to Wednesday and stop Thursday and start snowing again Friday good grief. I'll be so glad when spring gets here then I will be happy When my father in law was alive he was always having heart attacks and had to traveled to mountains to see him and had to drive very bad and slippery roads and was a nervous wreck. He had about eight attacks before him finally past on. I loved that man very much and miss him more and more every day. I think he has been dead about four years now. He was a world war two vet and has flags on his grave all the time. I am a Viet Nam war vet and am going to have a vet's funeral and want them to play bagpipes with the ceremonies My grandfather Elmer was also a world war two-vet. My Aunt Gloria had my grandfather cremated. I am from a military family and would go back to army if I were still young. Elmer was more like a father to me than a grandfather and he took pride when I was with them. When I was younger, we would go to this fruit market, the owner always said to me come here and would take me to back, and we would roast peanuts. The best peanuts were the ones he mixed salt with and you could eat shell and all. It seems that Archie always waited for us to get there so he could give me something.

We had a big family feud yesterday and its still going on today things are way out of control and wish things go back to the way they was.

Had to go pick up Jane at her work last night and got caught driving on snow and icy roads but made it back home safely.

Have no idea if anyone is going to work today will just have to wait and see.

When I was working I bought a canoe from a guy at work. One day decided to go out on river fishing. I loaded fishing gear in truck bought bait and six pack of beer. Put canoe on river and loaded all my gear into canoe and off I went. It was a real hot day and river looked like mirror so I decided that I did not need life jacket so I took it off. I rode across the river and up between the two bridges I went. I dropped homemade anchor over board so I could fill my pipe with tobacco and the damned canoe tipped over and down under, the water I went. Had no idea which way was up but felt canoe and it was moving and I held on and up we came. The canoe became wedged between two rocks and I began hollowing for help. It was about this time when river rescue came to my rescue and got me into rescue boat and other boats collected what to could gather from top of river. I was taken to Columbia side of river the guy from river rescue told me that a cop wanted to talk to me and was told this cop wanted to talk to me. At the same time WGAL, television was there and video taped everything that was going on. This cop was getting under my skin with all his questions and I said if you are going to arrest me do it and quite F—G around and he said if that is what you want that is what I will do. On went the handcuffs and into back seat of cruiser I went. My aunt called my wife and asked how Paul is? My wife had no idea what was going on. My aunt said Paul was on the six o'clock news . . . My wife had one hell of a time trying to find police station I was being held at after the incident. While I was in station, I asked the cops to take the cuffs off and they said not yet. I said to them I have no idea where I am at, have no shoes and am pissed, you all have guns where the hell do you think I can go. I sat in that chair and asked after cuffs were removed where my shirt is and the cop asks why. I told him my chewing tobacco was in shirt pocket. The cop replied your shirt is soaking wet and I said hell all the river water I drank and your worried about my shirt being wet, big deal. The one nice officer went and bought me a pack of gum. Police charged me with operating canoe while under the influence which cost me about two hundred dollars. After I got canoe back, I sold the canoe to my brother in law for fifty dollars. I had completely forgetting about all this until small game season when at lunchtime everyone was told that I was a movie star. My father in law had to show all the hunters that tape and I felt like a big ass.

Police were always chasing me home because I was always going to bars and drinking beer for hours. They would find me sleeping in my truck down at the river and would bring me home. Was at bar once and cops came after me and I got away from them and stopped at hardware store and bought spray paint and painted my truck different colors. This worked until they found out it was I and the chase was on.

My friend Ed and I were on our way to my in laws home and were talking to them by citizen band radio. I told them truck was running hot and pulled over off road so we could get out and piss. I heard this vehicle coming down the mountain road and decided to take a few more steps from road. There was this dump below me and down into all the junk I fell. It was raining and dark and has no idea how long I lay there. I heard my father in law above and had to light my lighter to find chain thrown down to me. Jim said grab the chain so we can pull you out before cops get here which I did. The next day I asked Jim my father in law where my truck was at and was told that it is at Joy's home. I found out that while I was down in the dump that Ed had put spring water into radiator and when truck was, being driven to Joy is that it froze up. Later when wrecker to garage carried truck, I found three pistons were in pieces and it cost about nine hundred to get it fixed.

Am going back to Korea now because it was a very interesting country. When I first got my unit in Korea, it was called the twelve Calvary units. Not long, it was change to the Indian Head Division so that they could send the Calvary unit patch to Viet Nam. I was then in what was called the 38th. Infantra Division because we were on the 38th parrell. The, winters were very cold and snowy, and I really hated them. One time we were playing war games and I was carrying a radio for communications on my back and was following this second leutenet. We was running down this finger of mountain when he lost his footing and fell and landed on his m 14 rifle and broke the stock. He had a very unusual look on his face and then began laughtening. Later on the same day the same day the same thing happened to me and all hell broke out. He called me all sorts of names and I said it was okay for him to break a stock because he was an officer and that I would get a court marshal because. He then wised up and said he would forget about it and call it an accident.

After a while air strikes were called in and the jets flew right over our heads using machine guns and then flew around and then flew over again and dropped napalm bombs of suspected enemy targets what a sight that was. We were giving these simulators which took place of hand garnades. They were made of plastic and had a cord which you pulled and when you heard a pop you then threw it and it would blew up. I was being giving orders over radio and happened to look back and saw fires all around and called this in to commanders in charge. I then got orders put out fires and yelled by mouth to fellow troops to come put out fires. There was always something interesting going on in my unit. I took pictures all the time over there and would go to hobby shop and develop my pictures. There was this fellow named Simmons who was always there and this one time was working on this plane and talked me into building one. The plane Simmons was working on had eight engines in and mine had only one. I was told I had to break in engine by mounting it down and to run it forty hours to get all the bugs out of it. After this, I put engine on my plane and we went up to battalion headquarters' field for flight. All the officers were watching from headquarters until my plane crashed into ground and they all disappeared. That was the beginning and end of my plane flying days. Simmons never got his plane off table because my time ran out and had to leave Korea.

All the soldiers in the army were told do not take pictures of bridges, airports or anything else because enemy if they got hold of these pictures could use time in time of war against us.

We were out on this mission and I really got sick, went to first aid vehicle, and was giving pills. I went back to my post and was popping these pills and next thing I knew woke up in my bunk. I found that I had taken too many and my stomach had to be pumped out.

I met many wonderful guys in the army and would like to visit with them all again for a reunion. I have a year book from Korea with names and addresses and wrote to several but never got any repely. I don't know if they went to Viet Nam and got themselves killed or what happened to them.

One time my wife was at work and my son Dustin was out with one of his friends. I was sitting at table drinking a can of beer and in walks my boy holding a finger to his lip. I said to him why are you walking around holding a finger to your lip and he starts. Its only a little scratch dad, he says. I asked him to take his finger away and out shoots blood. I said go in bathroom and run cold water on it which he did. After some time he returns and said the cold water will not help. About this time in walks my wife and says what the hell happened to you and Dustin says mom its only a little scratch. My wife says to me take that boy to emerengy room he needs stiches. I took Dustin to hospital and the doctor had to put three stiches inside and about five outside. The doctor asked Dustin what happened to you and Dustin told hime he ran into a barbed wire fence.

There was this time when I was out deer hunting and my wife called her mother and asked where's Paul ?Sis my mother in law says Paul and everyone is up on hill hunting. They started hollowing for me and we all went down to find out what was going on. My wife told me Dustin had been hit by car and was on his way to hospital. Jane then asked me to come home and I told her the whole mountain was solid ice and that I would come home the next day. The next day I drove home and Dustin had received a broken leg and many other injuries. They kept him in the hospital several days and went to my aunt and uncles home because they didn't have all the steps to climb. We left Dustin stay there and my aunt tutered him so that he would pass at school.

Everytime Dustin turned around something would happen to him it about drove his mother Ethel crazy but we made it through.

My son moved to North Carolina to be with his brother and hes still living there now. He has a good job and he got married and they have two sons now. Him and Heather his wife and the two boys are coming to visit us in Febuary and I can't wait.

Then there was this time a bunch of us were at work talking and it was brought up that the KKK was holding a sayonce at Ramires Hollow and we decided to be noisy and check up on them. We all met at a bar in York bought beer and some other stuff and went to this hollow and got out of car. I had my pistol and my flashlight and we was walking up this road and I stopped and said what the Hell, I turned around and all the chicken shits that were with me was gone. I got back to my car and there were inside and wouldn't let me in. Thank god I had my keys in my pocket. We never located the KKK but we had a very interesting night.

One time when I was stationed in Germany was at service club and was asked to sign this paper to go skying and I said okay and signed the paper. On sat I went back to service club with three friends of mine and off we went to this ski lodge. The farther we went up this road in the bus the more snow we came upon. The name of the place was Hitlers Monistary and it was very interesting. When we got out of bus we decided to eat first which we all did. In the back of restaurant there was this big wooden tank and we were giving mugs and got our own beer. After I filled the mug with beer I held it up and the beer looked like oil and could not drink all that beer. We never got out to ski because we went sight seeing and throwing snowballs and had to much other fun.

I met this German soldier and he and I went to a german club he knew and we ate german food and drank german beer. I learned some german songs that day and had much fun. drinking beer and stomping my foot. We then went out taking pictures and had fun climbing in and out of burned out military(German) vehicles and going through an old German cemetery. I spent much time in Fulda and Frankfurt, Germany and saw many interesting things.

I remember this one time grandpa, grandma, mom. dad, George, Gloria, and me went up along the allegheny river camping. We rented two cabins right near the river and the next day gramps and I loaded the fishing gear into motor boat. I was about nine years old then and loved being out there fishing with my grandfather. Gramps put one of his favorite lores on this pole and casted it out for me. He handed me the pole and told me to hang onto it which I did. He got the boat moving in trolling position going up river and then down river. All of a sudden it felt as if the line was snagged and pap says you have a big fish on the line. Gramps then told me to reel in the fish and as the fish came very near to the boat gramps said wait until he can get the net. I being very excited grabed the fish line and this big musky jumps off the hook. My grandpa was very sore at me and he told all his friends what an ass he had for a grandson.

One time gramps and I went fishing near Freeport dam using home made doe ball. We had an agreement that when someone got fish on line the other would reel in his line. There was this tug boat pushing these barges through the locks when all of a sudden grandpas line starts going out. Gramps picks up his pole gave a jerk and snags this fish. I hurried and reeled my line in and gramps says here you land the fish. After a long battle with this fish I finally got fish near shore and looked for a place where there wasn't any big rocks. I had the fish near shore and reached down and got the fish and had my hand up under his gells and lifted fish out of water and the fishes tail was still on the ground as I stood up. I then asked all the fisher men that were there if anyone wanted this fish and they asked me what kind of fish it was. I told them it was a carp and nobody wanted the fish so back into the river the fish went. This was truly the biggest fish that I had ever caught and at last gramps was very proud of me.

One night mom, dad, George, Gloria and I were up at our cabin near Tidiout, Pennsylvania in bed sleeping. About two in the morning dad heard these sounds outside the cabin and running around inside the cabin with a broom to protect us from whatever was outside. We later found out from my grandparents when they finally arrived at the cabin that nuts had been falling on the roof. That was the noise dad heard durning the night.

Dad had a friend that was at a camp ground not far from where we was at and decided to make a trip to visit and go fishing. When we got to this place Bert Bowser and his wife and family greeted all of us and said he had the ideal fishing place. To get to his spot we had a long walk through areas that if water was running high we wouldn't be able to walk there. We had to make noise when we were walking because there was snakes rattle snakes and copper heads around. Whe we got near the place we had to cross part of the river to reach this island. As the day went by and evening began moving in the water on that island began to disappear. mom said it was time to head back to their tents so off we began. We had to walk through part of the river and mom was carring one of the twins when all of a sudden she screams that a big fish or water snake went between her legs. We stayed with the Bowser family and the next day went fishing again and mom caught the biggest cat fish I ever saw and we kept it. When we got back to our cabin grandpa and grandma were there and wanted to know where we had been. Elmer said to Pat what are you going to do with that big fish?And mom told her father he could have it but he said he didn't want it. Elmer knew a guy down the road that had a cabin with a pond so him and I went and through the fish in his pond. One time after that we stopped to see Charlie and he told us about the big fish in his pond. Neither one of us told Charlie that we had put that fish in his pond.

Another friend of Elmers had this gas station and store in Tionesta and he had a box with lights inside and always had many rattlesnakes and copperhead snakes in there. I spent much time standing there watching the snakes crawing in side of that box.

This on summer vacation we took my wifes sister Judy camping with us. We went to this camp ground near Taylors Island in Maryland. The next day we all went fishing and Judy has a bite and began reeling in her line. All of a sudden she lets out a scream and the fish pole goes flying and there goes Judy heading for the tent. I pick up the pole and when I got the line almost in found an eel on her line. That was the last time she went fishing with me. Durning the night we had a ral bad storm and our tent was blown down. The next day we had lines runnig alround to dry up all our clothes.

Another time I had vacation and decided to take my wife to the Okefanoke Swamps in Georgia which we did. We rented this motor boat and out into the swamps we went. I was operating the motor and Jane was in middle seat and gramps(Elmer)was in the front seat. I saw this alligator right along side of the boat and took movie picture of it. I took the oar and poked the alligator on the back and he went under water. All of a sudden his tail comes up out of the water and then slams his tail down on the water. The boat almost tips over and my wife got very excited and told me lets get the hell out of that area. That was the last boat ride we went on in the swamps.

We spent that night there and my wife and the old man had fun feeding the buzzards and sea gulls. That night I kept hearing noise outside and would open the hatch and shine flashlight to see what was out there. After many attemps I found out what was making the noise. There was a mother raccoon and her babies inside of this grocery bag eating our cookies and some other goodies in that bag.

I had a Pinto station wagon and coming home the car was making weird noises. I pulled to side of road to check the noise and this Georgia smokie pulls up and the trooper asks me the problem. He told me to follow him that there was a Ford garage up the road. The macanick raised the car and when he took cover from pumpkin all these gears fell out. He said he would get the parts and sinse warrenty was still in affect it wouldn't cost me anything. We found this restaurant and motel combined and got a room for the time we spent there. We where in the resturent eating and it was raining outside. There was pots and pans all around in there and water was coming through all these holes in the celling. In our room the phone did not work, the tv wouldn't work and the air condishaner didn't work. It seemed ever time I walked down to the garage the rain would start. It was two days we were there before my car was fixed. On the way home we took a ferry boat ride and was feeding the galls and I was taking home movies of this. We had a lot of fun traveling with my grandfather. he was such fun to be with. On our way home came upon a deadly car accidenr. This sports was completely torn apart and they were trying to land medicvact helicopter. There was too many power lines in the area so they really had trouble but finally landed.

When I was a boy I liked playing cowboys and Indians and we had much fun. I always wanted to be a bad cowboy so I could go around betting up people and robbing trains and banks.

I met this young girl by the name of Kathy and really was and still am n love with her. We would go swimming in the Allegeny river and have such fun. I would go to her aunt and uncles home and really have fun. Her and her mother was having family problems and I tried helping Kathy out. Kathy moved to Sharon, Penna. And I went to visit her and found out that she had a new boyfriend and it pissed me off. I went bowling with them and wanted so bad to through the bowling ball at her boy friend. Him and I was fist fighting on and off. It got to the point where I caught a bus back to New Kensington, Penna. I also found out that she had a baby and often wondered if the baby was mine or not.

I also had a girl friend called Sandy and her older brother was in the army. Frankie was away with the army and Sandie was driving his car. Sandy was mad at me and this one day I shoved potatoes up the tail pipes of the car. I was watching from a distance and out she comes and gets into the car and starts the engine. All of a sudden the car makes one hell of a bang and potatoe bits fly everywhere.

This is the story of a person by the name of Paul A. Ramsden born on Feburary 25 1946. My mothers name was Patricia L. Leiter. Daughter of Elmer and Rose Leiter who lived in New Kensington, Penna. I was born and lived with my grandparents along with Pat until about age four when mom married this guy by the name of Thomas J. Ramsden. My real dads name was Paul Hartman and Inever got to meat him because he was killed at work by fire and explosion.

One time mom, dad, my aunt, my uncle and some neighbors were swimming at the creek below our hill. They held their noises one at a time and as they were running towards the water would say one, two, three and jump into the water. Mom said all of a sudden their I went and did the same thing and into the water I went. The grown ups then had to find me under water and bring me safely back to my mother. They then built a fire to dry me before my granparents found out or there would have been hell raised.

One time mom was cleaning house and I wanted to visit Elmer and Rose down the road from our house. My took off all my clothes and had front door locked. I just happened to able to unlock the door and out I went. The only thing I was wearing was a pair of red slippers and mom caught up and that was the end of that.

My brother and sister were born eight years after me. They were twins and mom really had her hands full with them. It was hell on me because they got away with everything. I had to share my toys with them but I wasn't allowed to play with their toys. Gloria was born one and a half hours before George. Gloria was Toms angel she could do no wrong according to him and always got her own way. All the neighbors were like one big family. You knew what they were having for supper and just about everything else that was going on in the neighbor hood.

I had many friends but liked some more than the others. We ran the neighbor together we took turns eating at each others homes.

We had this huge ball field where we could play football, baseball of whetever we wanted to play.

My sister came home from school one day with this huge dog pulling him with a rope and said mommy can we keep Teddy he followered me home from school. Tom had a hell of a time getting rid of that dog.

I remember this time the older teenagers had this cat in the woods trying to kill it. I captured the cat and put it under my shirt and off I went to my home. I told mom what was going on so we kept the cat but what a mistake that was the cat shit and pissed everywhere.

This one time Frankie Mitcheltree and I had sticks and was hitting rocks and I told Frankie not to get so close because I didn't want to hit him on the head with my stick. This one time I threw this rock up and swang and hit Frankie on the head and there was this nail in the stick which put a hole in Franks head. My step father rushed him to the emergency room and got him patched up. We had this neighbor that had a retarted daughter which I hated. My friend and I was sitting between the two houses and Katty was standing there and I told he to get away. She gave me a hard time saying I live her and you can't chase me away. I then picked up a brick and told her that if she didn't leave that I was going to throw the rock through their kitchen window. She would not leave so away the rock flew right through the kitchen window right into a pot of spegetti her mother was making. Boy did I ever get my ass kicked that time by Tom, and him and my friends fathers had to pay for that damned window.

Tom was adding a front porch to the house this one time and had the blocks in place. He had broken a hole through the wall and had not put flooring over the porch yet. Pat told Tom to go catch the chicken and she would make supper with the chicken. Tom and I went into the basement and Tom got a two by four and put four nails into the board. He then got this chicken and told the chicken to put its neck down so he could bend nails over the chickens neck. The chicken had better ideas and got away and ran through the hole in the wall. The chicken then got out in the yard and Tom and I were chashing the chicken all around the house with a hatchet. Wonder what the neighbors thought when they saw what was going on. We caught the chicken after awhile and ate it for supper and the chase was well worth the effort.

This one time I was down at grandmas house and she was about to light the oven. She turned on the gas and when she opened the over door out runs the cat with smoke coming from its fur, what a sight smoked pussy. The cat after so time turned out to be just fine.

When a holiday came around my grandmother Rose cooked everything you could think of and I ate like a pig. Gramps had this back room and he kept it locked from me. Right before Christmas he called me into this room and showed me the train display he had and said merry Christmas. It was a plywood platform with this lionel train all fastened down and everything worked. The train had a whistle and when you put a little white pill in the smoke stack white smoke came out. I played for hour with my train and had much fun.

This one time we was at the cabin and gramps said we had better start for home before the roads got to bad. Elmer had a Studiebaker and Tom had this big chysler. We was going up this mountain road and the back wheels on the chysler started spinning all of a sudden up the road comes gramps with his studiebaker car and pushes the chysler up the mountain. Everytime Elmer told the story to somebody Tom would really get pissed.

One time Elmer and I went up along the river and while he was fishing I threw the can of nightcrawlers into the water and really caught hell. That was the end of that fishing trip.

There was a fire at the Camp home and old man Camp died in the fire. Granmother was pissed at Tom. When the fire trucks came up road Tom heard them and jumped out of bed. He jumped out of bed and ran out to see what was going on. Tom was worried about himself and no one else and grandmother never forgave him for that stunt.

When I was still in the crib I found out that if I stood in one corner and shock the crib the screws worked them selves free and the bed would fall. I then would climb out and onto the floor I would crawl.

My grandfather had this big garage and many tools. In the garage he had a rowboat that he had built turned upside down on these horses. My friend and I were in there one time and we built a fire under the boat and my great grandfather caught us and said he would tell Elmer. When Elmer came home from work his father told him what I had done. I then saw Elmer coming my way and I ran to hide. It didn't work Elmer got a switch from this tree and when he caught me used that thing on my ass. I cried all the way room and when I told mom about it she said good for you, you needed it.

Grandfather always had a big garden and would grow just about everything you could think about. My grandmother would can just about everything that grew in the gardens. Grandmother would also bake and make bread and all sorts of good tasting things.

When I was going to Martin school I rode to school on a school bus. Sometimes I would ride this other bus that only went to the hill above our home. We then had to walk down this steep road. There was this farm to the left of the road and we would throw rocks into the field. This one day Silvio and I were throwing rocks and old lady Milko saw us. She got her shotgun and began shooting at us and the pellets began flying all around us. We both jumped over the fench on opposite side of road and crawled home through the woods. We was scared to death that time but it never stopped us as we kept on doing it.

There was this time Silvio brought caps to school on the bus and we were using our thumb nails to set them off on the bus. There was this patrol boy on the bus and told us to stop and we didn't. The patrol boy told the school principle about this and after I got to school and was in class the principle came to our rooms and used a ping pong paddle on both of our asses.

Silvio brought dog biscuits to school and we was eating them on the bus. Again this patrol boy caught us and again we got our asses beat with the so called ping pong paddle.

They had this glue that had a good smell and also taste good to eat. My teacher told the priniciple and again the paddle was used on my ass. When I was in third grade I fell in love with my teacher boy was she ever pretty. Why did so many bad things happen to good old me?

My brother and sister were born December nineteen fifty four and they were twins. Gloria was born about one and a half hours before my brother George. It was great to have some body to take care of. Mom had her hands full but Rose my grandmother was always around to help out. They had all these was lines running everywheres and was always full of diapers drying.

Gramps heard that there was land for sale to build cabin on at Tionesta. Elmer and I went to Tionesta land office and talked to the people and Elmer ended up buying a section of land

and we built a three room cabin. We all pitched in and before long the cabin was built. We spent many wonderful days and hours there. Down the road about four miles was the Nabraska Bridge where we could go fishing. It was part of the flood control project and from time to time the water would back up closing the road. There was this dam near Tionesta that controlled the water level at Nabraska Bridge. Elmer had a home made row boat that we used there and a few years later he bought a sixteen foot aluminium boat with a five and a half out board motor. From the bridge it was six miles to the dam and the fishing was out of this world. There was talk about the core of enginners building a dam at Kinzu, Pennsylvania. There was these indians living up in that area and they had to relocate them to another area. The indiand put up a hell of a battle but lost out. The United States government had to dig up the Indian graves and re bury them at Senneca. Pennsylvania or New York. We would take rides from time to time to check up on there progress at the dam site. It was a fantastic sight to see all the big digging rigs and trucks running all around. None of our family has ever put a boat on that part of the river.

I was still going to Martin school and there was a store up the road and I would buy baseball cards with gum in. I would then go to school and would pitch the cards at this wall. The card closer to the wall would win. If somebodys card was against the wall and your card landedon their card you won all the cards. If someones card was close to wall and you threw card and it stood against the wall you would win. We did the same with marbels but made a circle and had to shoot and knock marble from the pot. Some times I would win either at marbels or cards and with all those marbels sometimes they would fall out onto the floor. The teacher would get pissed and end up taking them and wouldn't give them back.

It was snowing this one time and there was snow already on the ground. We all began throwing snow balls at the girls and the patrol boy caught us. He took our names and again the priniciple came up the hall way and each one us got beat by that ping pong paddle again. I would get my as beat at school and Tom would beat my ass again for the same thing. I eventually graduated from that school and went to Ridge Avenue High School. I took up wood shop and made many things from wood. I was always on the shit list with some of the teachers and they used bigger and stronger paddles, ask my ass it knows. We were in nineth grade and were taking a test. The teacher told us no cheating and no talking and he was leaving the room for a while. There was this girl we called big red and she was caught cheating. The teacher went and got this other teacher for a witness and took big red out in the hall and beat her ass. Big red then came into the room laughing and the teacher said you think I am playing games and out she went again and that teacher really nailed her ass that time. She came back to the room and her face had a blank expresson on it. We used to take gym with the girls and would always catch hell from the coach because we would tease the girls. We used to have ink wells in top right hand corner of our desk. This one time I took top off of bottle and put the hair from a girl in front of me into that bottle of ink. Boy what a mess I caused. Tom found out I got my ass beat again and he had to buy that girl a new shirt.

When I got to this school there were blacks attending the school. This one time these black girls were getting smart with me and I called them Nigg—and they got really pissed. One of the girls was going steady with this basketball player and told him. I decided to go down stairs and sneak out side door so as not to meat up with this black dude. He must have read my mind because when I came out that door there he was. You talk about an ass whipping did I ever get one. I think that was the worst time I ever got beat that bad. After words he told me that if anyone picks on me just tell uncle Chicky and he would take care of it. For the rest of the time I was in school he took good care of me.

There was a lot of blacks in that school and I had many many black friends. There was some that were real pain in the asses and tried to stay away from them.

My mother has a younger sister and her name is Gloria. The first job aunt Gloria had was telephone operaror at the Bell Telephone Company in New Kensington. Pennsylvania. Mom worked at pet stores and such.

Thomas J Ramsden my step father had four brothers and three sisters. Their names are as follows Jim, Frank, George, Aggie, Ann, Julie and Joesefene. We were always going to family reunions and I always got into fights with my cousins. Some of the fights had to be broken up the elders. Since I lived in western Pennsylvania we would fight with our cousins from eastern Pennsylvania. The families had relatives with last names of Doctor Lipenski, Arbetiseski, Wisneski and these were on my mothers side of the family. It really felt good to had an uncle that was a doctor. Most all of them played some type of musical insterments and would stand around singing and dancing. When my cousin got married Dennis my other cousin and I got into one hell of a fist fight and my cousin Dennis ended up with a black eye and bloody nose.

Granmother and grandfather and I went to their cabin this one time. Gramps worked with this guy and had a tent set up and was sleeping with his wife and kids. Gramps pulls up by the tent and throws firecrackers at the tent. Later on in the day this guy came to visit gramps at our cabin and this guy tells Elmer that the mafia was out to kill him. That these guys were shooting machine guns at him. One time gramps had this big fish and laid the fish under the porch of a neighbor at the cabin. Sam our neighbor and his neighbor Johnny were always fightenning and Saw thought Johnny had put the fish under his porch and there was hell that time.

I was in class this one time and my friends were dipping coppenhagen snuff. I asked if I could try it and they said okay. Dam I was never that sick as I was that day. I threw up in school and all the way home. When I got home I told mom that I was going to lay down till supper time. Supper time came and went and I was still sick on my bed. Later that evening grandmother and grandpa came up and Elmer said good for you next time you'll know better.

I finally got out of Ridge Avenue hich school and into the senior high I went. This school was called Ken High and I took up machine shop. We had lots of fun fooling around with all those machines.

After school this one time Silvio and I was under the highway in this huge tunnel smoking ciggeretts. All of a sudden I look at the end of the pipe and there stands my grandfather and did I ever get my ass welted. Gramps said he saw smoke and stopped to check up and find out what was burning. It just seems that he knew when I was doing something and was right there.

Silvio and I were always up to no good. We would dam the creek to flood the road. We would breake holes in this huge septic tank so all the shit and water would run out. We threw snow balls and mud balls at everything and anybody. One time I came home from school and the phone rang. It was Mr. Miller on the phone and wanted to talk to my mother. Mom started raising hell on the phone and after she hung up the phone said. Mister Miller just accused Silvio and I for soaping his car windows. I called and told Silvio what was going on and he said he will be right over. He had soap and wax and away we went. We thought if we are going to be blamed for something we had better do something about it. After that there was no more phone calls.

Then there was this time this Jewish family moved up on the hill. My friend and I were walking home and I told this Jew that he wasn't welcome to walk with us. He just kept up the bull shit and it really pissed me off. I grabed holed of him and slammed him into this tree and told him to take off his shirt and pants. After he was done I grabed his clothes tied them it a ball and threw them up into a tree. Later that day this woman comes to our house and my mother told this women to get the hell off her porch and go home.

Silvio and I would climb trees and swing back and forth and really have fun. There was this black top road and my head hit the road and had to go see Doctor Lipenski and did he ever give me hell. The older teens had this bull rope for a swing. They had this big knot to sit on and this one day there was a lot of us up there. I was sitting on the knot and when I went in the kids kept jumping on and this one time off I went. I landed up side down in all this trees and had to be carried home. I was knocked out and again went to see the doctor and again caught royal hell. I was down in the woods this one day and saw Silvio and began showing off. I jumped from one tree to the next and the limb broke and down I went. Had these high boots on and when I pulled off the boot my ankle swelled and I couldn't get my boot back on. Silvio help drag me up the hill and then went and got his wagon and took me home. Again it was Doctor Lipenski that put the cast on my leg and he was not happy. One day after school this friend of mine said there is a carnaviel and we should go. I said lets go and while we were there it rained and my cast got wet. There was a steel bar on both sides of my leg and when the cast got wet the bar came out and the rubber bottom came up against my foot. My friend had to almost carry me home. When I got into the basement I climbed up on the work bench and put the bar in the vise. I then grab my leg and pulled the bar to place it was. I then got a roll of black tape and then electric tape and taped everything up. It worked just fine until I went back to see Doctor Lipenski andagain did I ever get chew out. The doc then told me that he never wants me back there again.

The older teens had this log from one tree to another and was about thirty feet above the ground. I was there this one time and was trying to reach the other end of this log and again down I went and away to the emergency room I went, yep doc Lipenski again and more hell he raised. when I had that cast on my foot mom cut my pants and put snaps on them so I get them on.

We would go down the bottom of our hill in the winter time and build fires. We used to ice skate on the creek and had to watch out for rocks sticking up. Ther was these big lights and we used to knock them out. This one time I threw this rock and the guy that worked at the high school caught me. He took me to the school and called my parents and my parents had to pal for that light. Yes I got a good ass beating from Tom that time to.

We were always building shacks in the woods and underground hide outs.

My grandfather was always buying me radios and this one time when they lived in the country he told me that he would get me a short wave radio. I had to help him with the work around the house and that is the way I got the radio. When I went home with the radio I strung wire between two glass insulators. That antenna really worked good. I would listen to Radio Moscow and the Voice Of America as well as many other stations.

There was these big tunnels under the high ways and roads and some were very long and dark. We used to dare each other to go through them.

My aunt Gloria would take me ice skating or roller skating with her. I had much fun when her and I was together. When she got married her husband James was in the navy. We used to go to Norfolk to visit them and would have much fun. Jim then went into the air force and this one time I got to go to Albuqurque, New Mexico with them. They had this pink and whiteford and had a u haul trailor on the car. On our trip we stopped at many interesting places. We had this eight millimeter camera and took movies all the across country. They played many tricks on me at the different motels we would stop at. My aunt Millie and my aunt Sophie lived at San Antonio, Texas and we stopped to see them also. My aunts were really glad that Jim and Gloria had brought me along to visit them. I also made trips there with my grandparents and also my parents and we always had much fun. I was at the Grand Canyon and about drove ny grandmother nuts because gramps and I were sitting near the edge of the drop into the canyon. I also got to see real Indians and buffalos. This one Indian talk me how to dance like an Indian and we have movie pictures of all of this.

This one time up at the cabin gramps make this bow then he made an arrow. He said this is the way the Indians shot their bows and puts arrow in position. He pulls back and lets go expecting the arrow to fly through the air but it just drops on the ground. We all got a big laugh out of that.

M grandparents were living with my great grandfather at main street in Parnasses, Pennsylvania at this time. My great grandfather had to use two canes to get around. He used to trip me with the canes whenever I walked near to where he was sitting. I enjoyed going to visit them because there was secret passage ways and secret rooms to investigate.

My grandparents heard a thud this one time and found Oscar my great grandfather lying dead on the bathroom floor. He had a very nice and large funeral with many of his close friends there.

My grandparents found another house for sale at Saxonburg Road and they bought the house. The home was located out in the woods away from town. It needed lots of work done to the house and I would spend most of my time there. Elmer and Rose planted a huge garden and grow just about everything you could think of. Gramps planted about thrre hundred head of cabbage and the groundhogs ate all but five of them. Elmer would buy traps and would set them in every ground hog hole he found. There was these old trees up in the woods above their home and the crows would land there. I used to get the twenty two rifle and shoot at them but never got any. From time to time we caught ground hogs in the traps. We would dig the hogs out and then shoot them with the rifle. I then had the job of skinning them and soaking them in water and vinager overnight. The next day grandmother would make them for supper and they tasted very good. By this time they had sold the house on main street.

When I was out at grandmother and grandpas house I would get the twenty two rifle and a bag of shells and walk down the dirt road. There was ponds along the road and I would shoot cans and things floating in the water. This one time I met Becky Briggs and I was always going to visit her and the rest of her family. This one time I took here to an in door movie in Leechburg to see West Side Story and she cried most of the way through the movie. I had my arm around her to comfort her through the movie. I would say that I was falling in love with Becky but things changed because I joined the army and that was the end of our romance. Right before I left for the army there was this black snake living in grandfathers basement. The snake used to lay on the cement block wall above the workbench with its head facing towards the work bench. My grandparents had many interesting things living in and around their home. I went deer hunting there but never got a shot at any deer. There were many rooms in that house and upstairs there was a secret room and passage way where I spent many hours. While I was away with the army grandmother and grandfather found a piece of ground up on Park View Plan number three hill near my parents. They bought the land and began building a home up there. When I came home on leave I would help them with their new home. After a large rain storm the back basement wall caved in and I spent many hours digging that mess out and rebuilding the wall. On the week ends we would get into Elmers car and go to the cabin to fish and hunt. I was home on leave one time and went to a dance where I met Elaine Grimes my first wife. We had gone out many times and wrote and asked her to come to Virginia Beach Courthouse and we were married. We lived at Robin Hood Apartments near Norfolk airport. At night when planes were landing the lights would light up our bedroom. After I was discharged from the army we moved in with my grandparents until we found an apartment of our own. I got a job in a steel mill called Shim Steel inNew Kensington, Pennsylvania. Elaine knew a girl friend living in a mobile home near Butler, Pennsylvania and soon we decided to buy one which we did. I would take Elaines younger brother George fishing from time to time. This one time there was four of us up along the river at night fishing. I had a cartridge from a pellet gun loaded with match heads. We built this launching pad from rocks lying around. I told George and his friend to find cover which they did. When they were ready I lite the fuse and then fell over the log, the next thing I heard was a very large explosion and a bright flash and could hear the rumble down through the canyons a long ways off. When we got home Elaine found out what I did and I again caught royal hell. I then got a phone call from Patricia my mother that my grandmother had died. When we got to grandfather home my grandmother was still in bed and Elmer was waiting for the undertaker to get there. My great aunt Millie was flying in from San Antonio, Texas for the funeral and everything else. I had to drive to the Pittsburgh airport to pick up aunt millie. Grandmother had a very large and wonderful funeral and I cried all the time. Grandfather after awhile sold the new home that they built and moved in with us in Butler, Pennsylvania. I was working at shim steel and was always being laid off. My grandfather and I drove to York County to visit my aunt and uncle. My uncle Jim took me to York Hoover Casket Company to put a work application in. I was in progress filling out this form and the personnel manager came out of his office. He saw my uncle and asked Jim if he was looking for work. My uncle Jim told Mr. Miller that his nephew Paul was looking for a job. Mr, Miller called over to the metal shop and asked the foreman there to come to his office. The foremans name was Charlie Godfrey and he showed me what I had to do. I liked the job very much and began working the following Monday and was there with that company nearly thirty years. I was standing up caskets this one day and pushed to hard and they all fell over on the floor. Ray Miller my best friend there heard the noise and came running. Ray saw the boss coming and said promise me you wont raise hell with Paul. Mr. Godfrey said he would be cool about it and he was. One time the water in the spray booth over flowed and water ran through the floor boards down to the next floor. The boss from that floor came up and really raised hell. There was many times after that we flooded the floor below. This one time this guy by the name of Guy Smith was sleeping in the coat room before our shift started. I found this long pipe and threw it onto the floor close to where Guy was sleeping and he shot straight into the air.

This one time Guy told me that he had a real bad headache. He was operating the elevator and went to take a piss. I ran over and into the elevator I went and I got inside a casket and closed the lid. When Guy came back he closed the outer steel door and then pulled down the wooden gate. As the elevator began to go up I opened the casket lid and yelled at Guy. I thought the poor man was going to have a heart attack. Then one time Guy told me he had a bad headache. After he got into the elevator and closed the doors I ran over picked up a metal bar and hit the door. It made a very loud noise and before long the doors open and out comes Guy holding his head. I always warned him not to tell me when he had a headache or else. This one time we were on our way to Florida and Guy was in the back of my truck laying down. I told Jane and Dustin to hold their ears and turned the eight track up as loud as it would go. Poor Guy almost jumped out the back of my truck. We got a camp site right on the ocean at Fort Augustine, Florida and it was a real cloudy day. I told everyone not to stay out long because they would burn really fast. My son Dustin and I went back to the camper and was planning to go deep sea fishing. My wife and Guy came back after some time and Guy went into camper and comes out with a winter coat on. I was really pissed at Guy and told him first thing next day we are going back home. On the way home Guy was sleeping in the back of the truck and we had a blow out on the camper. We finally made it home and took Guy Smith to the hospital. Later found out that he had second and third degree burns to his feet.

I would go to this one bar and took Guy there with me. This one time on our way to my home we stopped and Guy was drinking all sorts of drinks. When we got home Guy and my wife Janey went bike riding. I was at home drinking a beer and Jane came home and told me to call 911 because Guy wrecked the bike. Everything turned out just fine.

There was a rumor that the metal shop was going to close down and that I was being sent to wood shop. I worked there for some time and another rumor went around that we would be moving out to Emigsville, Pennsylvania. The rumor came true and we were sent to the new location. I guess that I worked at that location about fifteen years. I was moved from one position to another during my time there. Right before my illness I worked in glue area under Keith Stare. I really like working for Keith because he was a cool dude. There was three of us running this glue machine and William was always catching the machine on fire. We had more trouble with that wood in the machine than you could shake a stick at. William had a nickname for our boss and called him numb nuts.